Wings from Roots

Kathy Ellis, the second book of poetry

Previously Published, Awarded, and Special Works

"Addiction" was published in *Reach of Song*, Georgia Poetry Society, 2017.

"A Force / Uma Força" was published in *Reach of a Song*, Georgia Poetry Society, 2015, *Primero* by Kathy Ellis, 2017, and in Portuguese (traduzido por Rosangela Zanatta).

"All the Dancers I Have Loved Before" was published in *Setu International Online Magazine*, February 2018.

"A Man and His Sign" was published in *Setu International Online Magazine*, May 2020, and was published in *Dissident Voice*, February 14, 2021.

"A Reporter's Job" was published in *Dissident Voice*, February 28, 2021, in an earlier version.

"Aunt Bernadette's Ghosts" was read at the Atlanta Unitarian Universalist Congregation's virtual program, "Frankenstein: a live reading", October 31, 2020.

"Blood and Beets" was awarded Third Place in the Margo LaGatutta Memorial Award, "Category One", Poetry Society of Michigan 2019, in an earlier version.

"Celestial" was read at the Atlanta Unitarian Universalist Congregation's virtual program, "Frankenstein: a live reading", October 31, 2020.

"Chihuahua Cheese" was published in *Reach of a Song*, Georgia Poetry Society, 2019.

"Diego's Honeysuckle Tree" was published in *Setu International Online Magazine*, May 2020, in an earlier version.

"Divine Gratitude" was awarded Poet Laureate for the Spiritual Living Center of Atlanta, 2019.

"Names Carry On" was published in *Setu International Online Magazine*, May 2020, was read at the Atlanta Unitarian Universalist Congregation's virtual program, "Frankenstein: a live reading", October 31, 2020, was published in *Dissident Voice*, February 21, 2021, and was published in *Michigan Poetry Society Five-Year Anthology*, 2021.

"Octaves from Above" was published in *Setu International Online Magazine*, May 2020.

"Sanctuary of Atotonilco" was awarded First Place in the "Welcome Aboard" of Ohio Poetry Day Association, 2018, and was published in *Peninsula Poets*, 2019, in an earlier version.

"Space Girl" was published in *Peninsula Poets*, 2017.

Story 4 of "Endings or Beginnings (Her Voice)" was published in *Reach of a Song*, Georgia Poetry Society, 2020, in an earlier version.

"The Trailblazer" was published in *Reach of Song*, Georgia Poetry Society, 2017, in an earlier version.

"The Uninvited House Guest" was read at the Atlanta Unitarian Universalist Congregation's virtual program, "Frankenstein: a live reading", October 31, 2020.

"Waiting in Line" was awarded Honorable Mention, *Reach of a Song*, Georgia Poetry Society, 2018 in an earlier version.

"Wandering Cowgirl Boots" was published in *Peninsula Poets*, 2018.

Copyright 2021 by Kathy Ellis, Sandy Springs, Georgia
ISBN 9798678465610

In memoriam

Aunt Marcle Kortier possessed extraordinary intelligence in the arts. Aunt Marcle, like many artists, struggled to fit into the world during an era of intense stigma for people who experienced emotional imbalances, for women in particular.

Table of Contents

IMPRESSIONS

NOT RIGHT

SHORTIES

ROOTS

Acknowledgements
Afterword

Wings

"Not all those who wander are lost."
J.R.R. Tolkien, *The Fellowship of the Ring*

Sanctuary of Atotonilco

The modest entrance that faces east
of the distant Jerusalem,
at the vortex of the surrounding landscape
of water springs and mesquite trees,
      unsettles the soul.
The image of the Holy Land
houses the Sistine Chapel of Mexico.
Serene earth-toned murals
and Father Neri's scripted meditations in clay-red paint
grace all space on rising interior walls.
Without pretense,
without gold.
Sincere.
Sacred.

Hundreds of years
Thousands of sinners
      mumble their transgressions,
      flagellate their bodies,
      fast their last drop
until the myth of penance is empty.

Blood and Beets

During the war in El Salvador,
some things were not learned by explanation,
                              common sense,
                              following the one in front,
                              keeping safe.

Instead
              I had to figure out the bizarre along the way,
                    move through the days when everything changes,
                    comprehend addiction to adrenaline,
                    recognize that youth was on my side,
                    know the dangers of my own naiveté.
Seeking truth
        and
Bearing witness
To civil war
            to malnourished children,
                  machine guns chattering in the dark,
                  helicopters in the dark,
                  curfews,
                  shriveled vegetables,
                  teenage soldiers pointing guns at you
                  because they don't know where else to aim,
                  nearly thirty journalists' lives lost,
                  the assassination of Archbishop Romero,
                  the rape and military execution of four nuns.

I stayed.

If We Can Make it to the Comalapa Airport: 1980

Military roadblocks require their own set of rules.
    I am not Catholic,   I pray like   a nun in despair,
                              clutching her rosary.
    Touching the amulet around my neck,   I dream my own rules.
                  Let us pass. *Holy shit.*
  Do not make eye contact with the *soldados*.   Take deep breaths.
    Pray.   Pray like there is no friggin' tomorrow.
                                    O merciful God.

The narrow road to the Comalapa Airport
travels in secretive guises,
a weekend trip to the family cabin,
a country road to a church service.
Thick canopies shade
the isolated two lanes and their sad ghosts.
Volcanic asphalt unravels into potholes under a rainy sky.

After a year in this war-torn country,
two foreign females hire a driver to get them
and their battered luggage to the airport.
The road offers no hint for the chaos waiting at the airline terminal.
A desperate scene from the movie, *The Year of Living Dangerously.*
Except real.
Real pandemonium.
Desperate arms waving and shoving.
Unheard words clinging to the stale air.

    We are lucky.   We have airline tickets.
      Our *Americanness*   squeezes by armed guards.
Others must fend for themselves.
      Our flight delays.   If we can just make it to Mexico City.

                                   O Jesus.

The next nine poems are about El Camino de Santiago, Spain, 2016.

Sharing Light

The first day on the *Camino*
greets dusk on a sizzling day.
My head leans back
to absorb the rambling stone steps
worn by centuries of pilgrims.
As the trail leaves the village,
the dim streetlights melt into darkness.
No one stirs.
"Oh Lord," I mumble.
My eyes see nothing but
a tree-lined sky of no stars.
I wait.
A passing Spanish family waves flashlights
like SOS signals from a ship.
Stillness of the black curtain breaks.
They check on each other like mama bear and cubs.
Even on me.
The daughter sheds her light
onto my path of
dips,
roots,
grooves,
creeks,
and
the divine spirit ever unfolding.

Spanish Women under a Claudia Tree*

Nostalgia revives under a claudia tree.
Four hikers stop for a plum-tasting spree.
Nonstop Spanish chatter as the juice
trickles like fine Chablis.
What a day they all agree.
Some of the best moments are free.

*plum tree

The Irish Men

Eight senior survivors
engage their cancer cells
on a pilgrimage.
Bright orange T-shirts hike
in a group,
in twosomes,
and never alone.
Walking sticks mark the steady pace
of their candid stories,
trials,
tribulations,
triumphs,
brotherhood.
They are jovial.
They show their pain.
They eat ice cream.
They drink beer.
They look into your eyes.

Ode to Bacalao

Cod swims on world menus.
No matter where you go,
Cod frequents any venue.
Prepared in a hundred ways,
Cod nourishes the soul.
From oceans deep,
Fresh to frozen, salted and dried,
The goodness of cod reaps in heaps
At many docksides.
Taste cod flaky, boiled, sautéed.
Or relish the fish baked and in stews.
Simple or gourmet.
Stuff empanadas to satisfy a few.
Croquettes are the best.
Bacalao is de rigueur of the sea's treasure chest.

The Trailblazer

We pass each other
like birds in a draft
on a trail in Spain.
I plead to keep up with her youth,
she hikes like there is no tomorrow.
Her rugged spirit
hosts an expressive white smile
although she does not smile.
Shiny, dark strands of hair tied back.
Almond eyes.
Young thirties
My curiosity catches up
with the mystery hiker at a café.

Well, I'll be...
The hiker is a Marine pilot stationed in Tennessee.
She confided that a priest advised
to be kinder to herself.
I nod.
God plays dice with us.

Our chat dreams of her future
like tresses of milkweed drifting
in the blue Galician sky.
Eyes brighten. Talk quickens
Her strength grows
orchids in cracks of rocks.
The pilot and I part with affection.

A village later, where the trail goes steep and narrow,
    I spot the pilot's smile of joy.
    Her ebony hair lusters in the country sun.
    Her kindness secures the fragile hands of a pilgrim.
        Both giggle to navigate the rocks.

Mr. Welshman

Slight. Fit.
Mr. Welshman hikes around the world.
He speaks like no other.
All five American women lean in
To understand his Welsh brogue.
He offers a salve to fix a blister,
Opens doors for the morning ride,
Makes sure the women are set.
He enters the vehicle
As he thinks about the next hike.

My Irish

i

Eight men walk their lives.
Four stop for a break along the trail.
Two keep pace with other pilgrims.
Two have found a place for scenic pictures.
As miles continue, one talkative man grows silent,
Pallid.
Please be well.
I wish his struggles to go away.

ii

The middle-aged couple,
Plain they were.
Solid as the earth.
Proud of their two boys.
We talk. Not much.
Comfortable.

iii

"The donkey is braying because of your American accent,"
He lilts.
"Really? I thought it was your Irish one."
So begins the afternoon of sharing the trail.
Lucky as any Irish,
I walk with the director of the Historical Society of Ireland.
We examine artifacts, water ducts, and ruins,
Barely identifiable along the way.
Technologies evolve from ancient to modern times.
Happy us.
We share ourselves because of a burro.

Waiting in Line

The serene man is not from Spain.
His shiny coal-black hair and copper skin
are indigenous to the Andes.
He lives in McKinney, Texas.
"My name is Carlos.
How many years you think I have?"
He asks.
I answer sixty-three, shaving five years to flatter.
"I have seventy."

We wait in the long line of pilgrims
for the coveted Latin certificate
of walking a spiritual *Camino*.
He leans on a shepherd's pole topped off by
a beach shell, a gourd, and other *milagros*.
He could be a Jesuit.
"Save my place. I pray in the chapel."
We chat more when he scurries back.
"Wait for me." Carlos rushes.
We finalize our certificates at separate booths.

As we head toward the double wooden doors,
I point toward the altar.
"I wish to leave something."
Carlos sits quietly on a nearby hard bench.
Our moments together become too intense.
He feels love. I feel guarded.

He pressures, "Let's have a cup of coffee."
Carlos accepts my answer with a warm embrace,
holding his cane of memories,
before he disappears down the cobblestone street.

Addiction

Serotonin   Dopamine   Endorphins
release their magic into my neglected cells
along the sweeping landscapes of the *Camino de Santiago*.
Dreams and sentiment
drip into my veins,
soft and quiet like a cat entering a room.
As substance abuse needs intervention,
the steering wheel of withdrawal returns me
into the fray of American daily life.

Like captive birds released:
      Señor Serotonin crawls out of my devoted hiking boots.
      Señora Dopamine extracts her sweaty palms
      from my walking sticks.
      La familia de Endorphins has the gall to shout
      good riddance to my hiking hat,
      crouching in a corner.
The braid of happy hormones hums
back toward the horizon of Spain.

The chemicals don't disappear from body or memories.
      No *señores*.
      Like a parrot on my shoulder,
      memories beg for beginnings.
      A thousand wings flapping
      agree that *El Camino Nuevo* is
      a worthy call for what lies ahead.
Again.

Of Another Camino

A traveler ventures
A camino in Spain.
Mayan ruins,
Marine life of Valdez Peninsula,
Starry skies of La Serena,
Bogotá's Incan gold,
Europe and Russia lure another traveler
Toward Slavic languages, Irish beer, and Saint Basil's Cathedral.
The two engage over
Wine. Art. God. The Past.
He rolls melodious words
On his lips.
She savors the sound with her tongue.
They travel the undiscovered,
Where two paths converge,
Where juices marinate in the finest oak,
Where senses arouse each fluid cell,
Where the skin wraps the body in a lush cloak.

YOU

Tú

'ant

Sie

Ti

您

Tbl

Você

Pandemic Poets

We are even more eclectic on Zoom.

The poetry readings take place
in the early evening hours of shifting light, dancing pixels and silhouettes.
One attendee is blessed by the Zoom gods;
a halo glows from head to shoulder.
Screens reflect a mirror to fiddle with hair,
as though no one sees but we all do.
Internal nostrils appear when the screen is propped in a slanted way.
ENTs would feel at home.
One listener changes location three times.
We become dizzy as she props us here and there.

A handful of video screens reveals divine hairlines,
bad hair on no-care quarantine days.
My screen understands.
Quilts grace a favorite recliner in front of a window with lace curtains.
I think of wooden shoes from the Old World.
The 1970's wallpaper comforts my inner flower child.
The cats! *Oy vey.*
I am dying to open my screen to show my two talented felines.

A couple converses in the kitchen, muted.
He walks by several times,
to wash a dish, find a dish, anything with a dish.
I suspect he is jealous of his wife's Zoom ventures.
It is delicious.

The video-off screens are largely on the second or third page of gallery view.
They remain silent. The cheap seats. You will find me there.
Poet names on dark screens are funky.
I want to post my poet name, *Kellis,*
or at least a brooding photo of a struggling writer.

I am not Zoom enough.

I am envious of backdrops that are busy
with disheveled colorful books on shelves.
Hundreds of my books are behind doors
or tucked in assigned places. I am rethinking.
                  BUT I save the best for last.
The mug with a hanging tea label contains another liquid besides tea.
Ingenious! I am thinking.

Gatekeeper, Gifter, Giver

His tall stance reached out like a jewel box of colors.
He pressed on with the agenda and tasks,
no guise or complicated masks.
He always smiled.
His poems reverberated the irony of life
and performed his magic.
Our small group talked of darkness.
Left space for laughter,
the unsaid,
the unwritten,
the unknown.

He tolerated poems of cats.
He didn't tolerate two poems during open mic.
He handed me an antique book in Spanish.
I handed him my first published book.
He smiled.

I saw Ron for the last time,
face pale.
Lower back ailed.
He hugged my healing bones.
We chuckled and critiqued my poem.
I knew these were precious moments.
As the depth of his eyes began to fade away,
he smiled.

To know Ron for a fraction of time
was to feel his generous slices
of love of all things.
A cloud covers the sun today.
I want Ron's smile back.

My Dear Sir

Silver and softness seep
to find me,
release me.
Your right hand reaches out.
Fingers uncurl into the absence of time.
Your left palm releases serenity
like doves in springtime.
A polygon of gentle light lingers
like a bath of honey,
quiet-like,
between two people
in newfound ways.
You hold me safe.
I fill your void.
I am not surprised.
As a grain of sand grows into a pearl,
magic makes sense.

Endings or beginnings… everything ends, but a door may not open

Story One
The aging soldier loses sight
Of the horizon.
Days lead to a worse life.
He once stood as a warrior,
A lion.
His heart suffers greatly.
Depression shows no end.
Suffering unfolds a hard fate
Of hard luck.
He tends his barren garden
Of mud and rock.
The end is unclear—
A matter of when.

Story Two
The young Dutch elm tree offers humble shade
for the young couple and their toddler.
Her generosity grows as the family grows.
"Share your iced tea, lawn chairs, and stories," she says.
 Her bumpy roots break ground like tentacles.
 Her coat of leaves breathes fumes from the nightly trash.
 She survives Dutch elm disease.
 She never complains.
One summer day she senses a shift in the wind.
From the deep earth vibrations to the tips of the highest leaf,
the Dutch elm gathers
the family under her rustling canopy.
She waits for their return.

Story Three
She feels sorry. She annoys you with your friendship.
 She is more vested. Both of you wished to live closer.

Your yearly messages are often touching. She is grateful for decades of memories and laughter.   You could always make her laugh.

     But you are busy.   Conversations were always about you not much about her.   No return calls from you.   She misses you. You took leave much sooner than she.   The stage curtains close as you disappear in the shadows.   She wishes you the best.

Story Four (Her Voice)
Sky looked bruised and low clouds drape,
Like neglected grey curtains.
The rug pulled from under me.
No place to land.
Death makes its own countdown.
I didn't know.

You asked me to stay, many times.
This time I heard. The change in your voice,
a voice that requested little.
I sat near your bedside.
You beamed like a little girl,
a mother reclaiming her daughter.
You became my child as we skirted the final days.
How was I to know?

Tongues of wind lash at my thoughts,
my voice trapped in a stone.
You voiced last words,
"Turn off the light," as you slid into a coma.
I, with my head on your bed,
held your warm hand.
Not knowing.

Story Five
Decades long. She waited to
replay your sweet song. Your
memories seeped into each other's dreams.

You were as before or so it seemed.
Tender kisses, teenage
ardor to explore.
Laughter in your teasing eyes, she
could never defy. She
felt you upon her
like waves of the sea.
Tidal swells permeated
her every cell.
She wanted to give everything to you.
Everything.
Her body hurt so.
Her pierced heart entered yours to
capture a time so pure.
You were true
until the end of it
all.

Story Six
He chose his lifelong,
Unyielding and headstrong.

Like his father's immigrant ways,
Father and son had a price to pay.

Land planted with corn,
Quilted by sun and sweat of scorn.

Boiled pain mixed with toil,
Over funds they recoiled.

Son escaped from the farmland he well knows.
Both held fermented memories close.

Father and son were left torn,
Leaving dragons in the wake to mourn.

Wandering Cowgirl Boots

Time to take off my wandering cowgirl boots.
I found me a long-legged cowboy.
I got some galloping unknowns to settle,
but
the touch of his warm hand,
like Indian summer,
tames the dust off this gal.
Cowboy Twain writes deep thoughts without corners
of showdowns, listless one-pony towns.
The man's imagination,
cold nights on the lonesome prairie,
cowboy caviar, aka black beans...
hankers to be hitched.
You done stole my heart, cowboy.
I don't want the broken parts back.
As stars rendezvous in western skies,
I found me a bright star out yonder to hang wayward boots.
Time to giddy up our stallions into sands and sundown
and
howl like wolves at a moonlit shindig.

Diego's Honeysuckle Tree

Twisted branches arch the patio wall,
    Frame a lace canopy
        Like the wingspan of a dancer's shawl.
           Flights of vitality.
Blooms blink pink with yellow tips,
    Flames of golden trumpets,
        Invite hummingbirds
           For sweet hours undisturbed.
Metallic green wings weave,
      Growing shadows float throughout Diego's magical tree,
        All while under the eternal rays
          Of the sun ablaze.
Blossoms and leaves blend into nightshade.
    Diego is gone,
        Deeper than roots that pervade
          His garden of Babylon,
But his memory shines
    Through the kitchen windowpane,
        Lying warm in my hands.
          Once again.

From Desert Sands of Old

He explores
The universality of
Languages.
Cultures.
Vocations.
Friendships.
Man.

He discovers silver and gold along the way.
Feeds his mind.
Experiences.
Seeks new answers to old questions.
Gentle,
Compassionate.
He nurtures others,
Blesses humankind,
No matter from where.
He is a treasure collecting treasures.

Walter of Miracles

Sagittarius. Taurus. Capricorn…
Grandmothers in *las cocinas*
put their lives on hold to hear
their daily zodiac readings from Walter.
Un puertorriqueño to the heart to the soul.

Clairvoyant, dancer, dreamer, healer,
the master of ethereal whirlwinds
from the deep realms of our universe,
Walter travels
with daring *cojones,*
his magnetic persona,
citrine capes,
glittery jungle-green jewelry.
He transcends the confused macho world.
The camera cultivates his miracles
of hopes and promises.

Walter and I share birthdays.
We tap into uncharted territories.
We share the depths of betrayals and joy.
We travel far but stay near.
Con mucho mucho amor, dearest Walter.

IN AWE

*"Awe is the feeling we get in the presence of something vast
that challenges our understanding of the world..."*

Greater Good Magazine

Divine Gratitude

The sense of gratitude opens
Heart–
Mind–
Breath–
Eyes.

Behold the showers of grace,
As natural as gliding wings.
The Divine grants our world
Completeness.

The bounty of blessings
Expands in our open hands,
Ever so abundant.
Ever so magnetic.

The morning light smiles.
Moonlight offers a renewed rest.
Starlight tenders a nest for a child.

Embrace us with your eternal light.

African Desert Rose

Splashes of crimson cherished by arid rays,
Succulent stems yield clusters of praise,
The African desert waited long,
Bursting into a perfect rose song.

Snow in Sandy Springs

White blanket of caress
Drops wintery kisses from the opaque skies.
Small wings appear darker,
Weave invisible paths in the white-grey,
Swoop through endless falling Stars of David.

Celestial

A sage moon looms
Its trumpets
In the spirited night sky.
Purple black holds a web
Of insistent muslin clouds,
Drifting like broken angel wings,
Beyond the reach
Of pagan haunts
and
Before the whispers
Of winter solstice.

The Wanaka Tree in New Zealand

When the water surrounds the Wanaka tree,
like an island in the sea,
mystery lures tourists and photographers
to capture the rare image.
The water recedes,
the strangers leave.
Tree leaves rustle.
A Māori native appears.
He begins to converse with the Wanaka.

The Māori is a recluse like his tree companion.
He sees the roots of the stark tree,
poised in a mystic lake expand
from its watery bed toward dry land.
No other roots join the Wanaka.

The sun streams light
throughout the sparse tree limbs.
The Māori transforms into a large bird,
perches on his friend's tender bark,
especially at dusk,
when he knows that two spirits stand content.

Flamenco Girl

Reveal your young self yet to flourish.
Reveal blossoms of pubescence.
Reveal unwavering movements.

Grace fingers, hands, and sweeping arms into provocative flame.
Grace feet into the depth of Mother Earth so she may bless you.
Grace your ripening body into an instrument of artistry.

Dare to swirl long strands into the air.
Dare to express your body without knowing its power.
Dare to stamp your art into the wooden floor.

Clutch your skirt.
Clutch your womb.
Clutch your naiveté.

Ignite your becoming.
Ignite kindling within your belly.
Ignite fiery Andalusian roots.

Embrace rhythm of thunder.
Embrace the bearing of carriage and swaying hips.
Embrace spectators' exuberance.

Dance the past into the light of fate.

The Nest above the Cottage Door

Mama bird flies into the glass door,
Falls flat.
Her chest releases
The last breath.
We five witnesses fall silent.

A Force

A violin echoes.
Strings pluck.
The solo dancer defies the tempo;
limbs and torso whirl into
the ethers of space,
raw and forsaken
like the chaotic currents of wicked winds.
Mysterious as the Mayan eclipse:
dance
solo,
Solo Dancer.

Uma Força

Um violino ecoa.
Cordas em pizzicato.
Um dançarino solo desafia o ritmo;
membros e torso rodopiam
aos éteres,
visceral e abandonado
como as correntes caóticas dos ventos malvados
Misterioso como um eclipse maya:
dança
solo,
O dançarino solo.

"The accident," the next five poems

Recall

I recall the sunny, cool day,
St. Patrick's Day, but no such luck.
My last memory was setting a plate on the kitchen counter.
I came to consciousness five hours later in a hospital.

No Recall:
Locking my house   Starting the car
         Taking a left on a busy road
             The hit
                   The screeches from brakes and tires
                         The air bags exploding
     My car sliding into oncoming lanes
                         Shock. Brain shutdown
Writhing in pain from the steering wheel dug into my pelvis, bones
breaking and bruises assaulting internal organs.

                 Fright, Flight, Fight!
                     The trio succumbed.
       The terror of the young man whose old car crashed into mine.
           He curdles the memory of the noises, sights, and trauma.
My car door cut off by who knows who.
      How did they ever get me out of that Mini Cooper?
     My endless stream of cussing.
           The backed-up traffic on an obnoxious road
               The one witness, the bystanders
    The policeman slipping the violation ticket with no defense into
my purse.
           The ambulance drivers
             The stretcher.
        The emergency room full of doctors, nurses, x-rays.
I recall the doctor who asked me if I had any drinks
            because it was St. Pat's Day.

Angels on duty:
The jogger, a first responder during the Vietnam war,
heard the crash during his run.
He held me down and elevated his voice over my resistance.
My unconsciousness asked my Muslim neighbor to pray for me as
paramedics slid me into the ambulance.
He spent the afternoon in the Mosque.

I recall:
The source of awe,
The kindness,
The giving.
Flowers that filled the hospital room.
The birdfeeder outside my window.
The medicinal Chinese soup and tea.
The healing tenderness of family, friends, nurses, strangers.
The brutal physical therapists.
The good things. The lucky things.

Disclaimer: I was not responsible for the nonstop obscenities in different
languages.

Prayers of a Moroccan

The Jaws of Life
peels the pockmarked car door
from my fractured pelvis and spine.
A man with spirit eyes, a gentle voice,
leans near me.
He witnesses the accident of mangled metal,
hears my echoed screams
striking the hammer on cold steel.
I am a delirious animal
trapped in a hunter's snare.
My subconscious strives to plead:
Pray for me.

He prays in the mosque with a thousand pilgrims from centuries past.
He prays until the protective mountains of Mecca engulf me.
He prays as though we are all one in this universe.
He prays all afternoon until he knows.

Gone with the Wind Staircase at North Fulton Hospital

Marbled, winding stairs,
Signature stairs,
Like inside an antebellum mansion.
One hand on the railing,
The other on the walker.
One stair.
My legs managed one more step.
Stairs were not ready for this dancer
Of fractured bones and deep bruises.
The staircase stared at me with ice
That melted in my eyes.
My walker wanted to whack the young physical therapist
Into "I don't give a damn" oblivion.
Real good.

Battle of the Bones

Pelvic bones twist
into melancholy.
Cracks echo,
      resist movement,
          retort their favorite obscenities.
               Bilateral acute fractures turn into misfits,
               limping in the sea of Pelvic Valley.
               Sassy right hipster joins evil forces with
               the worse crotchety left hipster.
Lumbar twins four and five on the sidelines
      refuse to rest their aches
          for the perfect timing
             to hurl their chilly grief.
               The friggin' hipsters
               cry out for Percocet
               but hone the bones with ibuprofen.
               Moans rebound
               within the invasive tunnel
               of *The Kingdom of M.R.I. Vader.*
The aftermath drags
      the bag of sorry-ass bones
          across the cold, empty parking garage.

Kitty Rocked the Ride

Four months later
Kitty blew in third.
Not bad for no sleep,
twice the age
of fellow spinners.
Five healing bones.
Rough. Rough.

IMPRESSIONS

"There are moments, particularly in times of stress, when haste does not make waste, when our snap judgements and first impressions can offer a much better means of making sense of the world."

Malcolm Gladwell

Octaves from Above

Wistful and carefree,
Flutes voice shyness in orchestras.
Chime their boldness in Mexican songs.
Flutes of gold, silver, jade, and bone
Touch octaves like hummingbirds weaving
Among blossoms of honey.
Flute notes channel vibrations
For the Queen Mother, Confucius,
Mayan farmers and cats in alleyways.

Flautist James Galway revels in Cleo Laine's jazz.
The heavens open. My musician mother
Sits with me during such performances.
She was the music.

Space Girl

So I am
at Carter's baby apparel,
browsing the buffet of pastels.
I am not a fashionista,
but I find the perfect get-up
for a six-month old.
In a heartbeat
my hands drop the girly, pink dress
for the violet-blue sleeper;
       glow-in-the-dark planets,
       spaceships,
       shooting stars!
Other possible worlds
exist for this girl child:
curious clusters
of the cosmos,
limitless discoveries
       in outer
and
       inner space.
I feel certain.
She's a space girl,
commanding her domain;
oblivious to the grownups' talk,
surrounding the shiny orbits
of her *Evenflo ExerSaucer*
from Walmart.
Three. Two. One.
 Blast off!

The florescent fabric reflects
the supernovas in her eyes,
illuminating the journey
toward the Milky Way.

Space girl travels deep
      into the galaxy
            of her universe, where
                  no human has ever gone.

A World without Jugglers*

A three-ball routine is a snoozer.
Throw five soccer balls, two folding chairs, and a saber into the mix,
jugglers grab slices of nirvana that Cirque du Soleil would die for,
playful except when the juggler gets wacked in the head
by a bowling pin or a runaway zebra.
You choose.

Jugglers' DNA strand
performs a close match to the odd whimsicality of
unicyclists, yo-yoists, magicians.
Busy Boy Scouts. The rootless. Introverts.
Loners who engage with strange objects
and understand gravity.

I have no desire to be around these bizarre characters,
unless they are from Russia or Eastern Europe.
They are smokin' hot.

* Inspired by Roger Easley's photograph on Facebook, January 12, 2020

A Gumbo Ingredient*

Cloudy whites fill the papery skin
of magenta lines,
bleeding like lipstick.

* Inspired by Roger Easley's photograph on Facebook, January 15, 2020

The Uninvited House Guest

We feel pockets of cold air
around our faces, tugs at our hair.
We lurch. Breathing surges.

The ghost alarms but does no harm.
His long white whiskers are annoyed, poor old boy.
I live in his place but
he puts up with me anyway.
I don't put up with his plaid blazer with brown elbow patches.
"Old school!" I yell, before he vanishes.

He often stands near the run of the stairs.
We know he likes it there.
The old man haunts one cat to run into walls
and chases his sharp claws
up the window blinds, just installed.

He gleans pleasure from scares.
I am not fooled by his perversions, anytime or anywhere.
The ghost needs warfare and crises,
and serious analysis.

There Is a Hijab in My House

She wears a hijab.
Loose clothing over fashionable tight jeans,
thong and high heels too.
Dark eyes command brother
to drive her anywhere on a whim.
She arranges how
and
what they will do.
She wishes to drive and swim.
She wishes a view from a high rise in Midtown.
How does she wish to travel the thorny line between:
   Land of the Tradition?
   Land of the Free?

All the Dancers I Have Loved Before

Yank out the rusty metal,
running down my spinal cord
spreading its darkness from neck to hips.
Frida Kahlo begs for release from her "Broken Column."
Ice releases water to flow
into her skeleton and mine.
She commands me,
"*Baila, gringita, con tu alma.*"
Pues…

Paul Taylor and I
share our liquid and light in *Esplanade*.
Our dancer wings fly away,
transcend into the cheeky sky of golden cherubs.
We are that good.

I limber with such finesse, that
Isadora Duncan is distracted from her drama.
My spirals flow into
soft currents and summer breezes.
She thinks I am that good.

Gene Kelly trampolines with me
beyond the burden of gravity.
Nothing like that feeling
of an oak tree full of branches.
Strong. Forever lasting. Wise in execution of movements.
He makes me look that good.

Cradled in Alvin Ailey's winged arms and tapered legs,
we dance praises
of the trinity of mind, body, and spirit.
We dance heavenly good.

The suave. tap. shoes. of Gregory Hines,
the daring. taps. of Michelle Dorrance
move like sonnets on fire.
My dream taps until flowers wilt in my hands.
Not so good.

Suddenly in the cluttered avocado-green kitchen,
an uplifting force of white light
infuses my joints.
Ricky Martin hot salsas my dancing soul
like there is no *mañana.*
So *caliente.*

Make Me Angels*

Weave me a carpet
> So magic flows sunsets of scarlet.

Float me in the seas
> So kisses fall from rain trees.

Paint me a masterpiece
> So beauty never ceases.

Grant me peace
> So wrongs are released.

Cultivate me into English landscapes
> So blooms open into magnificent shapes.

Savor for me the serenity of a magnolia tree
> So a hundred white doves rest on broad leaves.

Share with me secrets of alchemy
> So magical powers transform into reality.

Play me sonatas of cellos and violins
> So vibrations vibrations vibrations enter within.

Make me angels
> So their wings flutter like an accordion of paper dolls.

* Inspired by John Prine's "Angel from Montgomery"

NOT RIGHT

"Nothing can be truly great which is not right."

Samuel Johnson

Barricades

They breathe together
under the spell of unity
until it becomes truth.

They speak of their distaste of the outsider
or may not ever mention their name.
They share inclusion of the righteous.

They need to have the reins of control.
What they think they know
stems from their unaware selves.

Narrow habits pave
how to think and what to do
in the box of fear and resentment,

until there are no other ways.
They find comfort in the wall of sameness.
The outsider has little chance for membership.

Names Carry On

Untold memories exude from the simple stone
that rests atop the gravestone.
The Indian Mission Cemetery
haunts and echoes of years gone.

Crescent moons, sunrays,
raindrops under white-blue clouds,
painted on weather-worn crosses,
the buried lie witness to
silver lakes of bass,
deer herds,
laces of lichen,
velvet moss.

Ojibwa hearts carry on—
Chief Blue Cloud
Baby Nedwash
Hole in Sky
John Michigan
Squada
Unknown

Drafts in the remote cemetery
move deliberate and free.
The dream catcher,
fluttering from the nearby tree,
reaches for dreams.
Small flags upright in the damp humus
wave to war heroes
from these proclaimed forests
of long-ago chants and broken arrows.

A stone is not just a stone—
when the blood of a nation holds fast to a fading past.

A Reporter's Job

Reporting live from M.I.A. News!

Be on the lookout. A
young. White. Male
is angry.
Those mass shootings.
Tsk. Tsk.
The Lone Ranger attacks will get you.
      Just one time.
      Every time.
More than 250 other mass shootings in 2019.
Folks, we are only in the dog days of summer.

We don't have much to go on.
A Young. White. Male feels justified adding
another assault weapon to his arsenal.
Custom made.
Young white cronies congratulate him as if he had a baby.
Babies are not custom made.
Cronies ask for babysitting dates.
Listeners, we don't know *where* the next mass shooting may happen.

M.I.A. News knows with certainty:
the weapon comes home in
the wake of
The Dead
The Injured
and
The Traumatized
in El Paso, Dayton, and across this mighty nation.
Exercise extreme caution.
Repeat.

The Intent of Matter

Matter contains energy and substance.
We are of energy and substance.
Matter occupies space.
We occupy space.
What is deep within us matters.

Intent does not stand alone.
If intent is meant to be positive but
the impact is harmful,
the aftermath is unintended.
We feel sorry. Maybe ignorant.

If the intent is meant to be harmful,
the impact. triggers. reflexes.
      from the past
      from the depth of matter.
The ripple effects stream from darkness,
not from light.

We cease to acknowledge the other.
We hurt each other.
The relationship ceases to matter.
We feel we do not matter.

No matter.

The Flying Seagull*

His loopy walk, full beard, and lit smile
Heal children refugees' dark wounds
Into a somebody for the day.
Ash holds dazed toddlers
In his embracing arms as he prances.
Little legs follow him like Pied Piper
Down dusty paths away from
Daily harsh shadows of unknowns.
Games, magical tricks, music
Release scary creatures
Caught in their depraved sleep.
Ash flies to the next camp.
He leaves behind prized possessions:
Giggles.
Brighter eyes.
Pipedreams.

* Ash Perrin on YouTube

Whatever Happened to Adult Swim Time?

The lone swimmer's arms carve an invisible line
in the chlorine water,
claiming a sliver of pie.
Five screaming kids burst the pool gate,
invade the neighborhood pool
with cannon balls and chicken fights.
The swimmer is invisible to the two boys.
Water explodes into her eyes like fireworks.
Father admonishes the boys from his lounge chair
while entertaining his
jumbo QuikTrip iced tea,
Pringles,
something in a sack.
The neighborhood pool belongs to them.

Youngsters move around like dice in a cup.
They yell their banter.
They yell how to swim right.
They yell what to do next.
What does *real* yelling sound like?
The swimmer ceases her laps.
Her ears ring while she escapes through the gate door.
Father mumbles apologies for the commotion
as if he were never there.

Irony in a Few Seconds

Call when you need help.
She calls. Three times.
No answer.

I don't have a problem with your fiancé.
Were you supposed to?

He cried about his dead mother.
Family said he was weak.

God bless America.
Are you God?
Does God bless other places?

Resisting Covid-19,
armed protestors block the hospital entrance,
demand entrance to the Capital. Unmasked.
Images absent of police.

Peaceful protestors,
reporters mowed down, children pepper-sprayed,
mothers tear gassed by military.

A matter of color.

God bless America.
Which America?

We need to do what is necessary.
What about the native peoples?
Oh, there are only a few of them.

We believe in family values.
Do all families have the same values?

Be sure to keep in touch on your long drive.
Sure will.
No touch.

More lives would have been lost
if not for the nuclear bombs in Japan.
At least 140,000 perished.
The aftermath still impacts.

Doctor pulls straws on my health.
Four out of five are worthless medications.
Desperation harms.

What happens when there are no arms wrapped around you?
You must handle yourself.

"Hundreds of people haven't died after Hurricane Maria
as they did in a real catastrophe like Katrina."

Send her back.
To where?
Send him back.
Never hear such things.

Toxic thoughts
Toxic people
Are they intoxicated?
He is African.
There are more than fifty countries in Africa.

A teenager runs out of a store with a two-dollar beer.
He is shot dead.

Store owner: You must wear a mask.
Customer: Is anyone sick around here?
Store owner: Wear a mask.
Customer: You are not wearing a mask.
Store owner: I am drinking coffee and busy.

Monitor of a virtual meeting: "We are here to find out your point of view.
Everyone should mute their mics."

"We act without thinking
or
we keep thinking without acting."
Unknown

A state representative knocks
on the governor's door while he signs a bill.
She is arrested.

Irritations do not last forever.

Travel is a retirement dream.
Why wait?
Travel with less physical pain
or less of a chance of a heart attack.
Travel now.

Racism is as American as baseball.

Baptist churches are often segregated.
What's the difference in Baptist beliefs?

A Man and His Sign

Roads paved in gold?
Makes no sense in the land of plenty.
Your seven-year-old son struck.
By a stray bullet.
From a deranged gun.
I am sorry for your sorrow.
Hold your sign.
High.
The sign that holds the face.
Of your lovely child.
Let arms wrap.
Around your wretched pain.
You are here.
In the right place.
We hold your brokenness.
In a tender place.
Until the next time.
To march again.

SHORTIES

Writing a short poem can often be more challenging
than writing a longer poem.

A Vocation

Once a juggler always a juggler.
The Renaissance Fair,
The Ed Sullivan Show,
late-night programs,
festivals, conventions, casinos,
even sex shows.
Add a juggler,
and there goes your show.

Alignment

Keep spiritual prayers alive.
Keep the feeling all day
Of unexpected sweetness.

Dollar Stores

Cheap. Cheap, cheap.
Cheap. Cheap, cheap.
Cheeeeap all the waaaay.
Ohwhatfun
Itistobuy
One-dollar gifts today!

(Sing to the tune of "Jingle Bells")

Frenchy

He is everything French,
like a chocolate mousse enriched by orange liquor.
Frenchy is a quench to the thirst of her lips,
casting bouquets of spells and delights
as rare as trailing plumage that glides into her dreams,
shining like armored rubies
with a strength of a fortress.
She clambers his never-ending scent of temptations
while drifting in soothing waters.
They savor French wines from ancient vines and relish their stories.
Son prince Français.
Her French prince.

Reactions to a Word

Christmas
More Christ.
Yes, more Christ,
Not more gifts and sugar.

Holiday Season
Intense bipolar behavior

Shock Therapy
Wake up.
You are not enough.
You are too much.

New Year
Another chance
For more chances.

The Have nots
Hearts and desires.

The Haves
They think they do.

Exit
Ambiguity

Hanukkah
Nine lives
But different stories

Count
Why learn to count if we don't count?

"Imagination is having to live in a dead person's future. Grief is wearing a dead person's dress forever."
-Victoria Chang

Black Onyx

Imagination is having to live in the dead person's black hole. Grief is
wearing a dead person's black onyx ring forever.

Chihuahua Cheese

Chihuahua.
      Cheese.
            Queso.
                  Origin?
                        Mennonites.
                              North México.
                                    Semi-soft.
                                        Cow milk.
                                              White.
                                            Salty.
                                            Melts.
                                Supremo Brand.
                      Forms of Chihuahua Cheese:
                        Braids of Chihuahua.
                Balls of Chihuahua.
            Round wheels of Chihuahua.
          Blocks of Chihuahua.
      More Chihuahua Cheese.
Please.

Excuses

Beautifully crafted~
More wishbone than backbone~
Reasons why we say "no."
Cry me a river/

The Best Hair He Has Ever Seen

Dearest Black Bob Wig:
I love you. I imagine Uma Thurman in *Pulp Fiction*. I want to look like the Mia Wallace lady. The gobs of grey-streaked hair tucked under the perfect black bangs and bob for a night on the town. Oh yes.

He waltzes over for a dance. "You have the best hair I have ever seen." I have no chance to sit the whole evening.

Story changes with that black wig.

Winter Spirits

Royal orchids mingle with orchestras of starlight.
Crystals of snow grace plum trees.
Frost on glass sparkles like floating amethysts.

Clan

Unsettled covering
Disguises gentleness.
The blanket whispers
Thunder in dark rooms.
The plenty to hurt me.

ROOTS

"Give the ones you love wings to fly,

roots to come back,

and reasons to stay."

Dalai Lama

Our Dinner at The Priory

In the land of lamb and fish,
I ate fish every day in Wales.
When I was a toddler,
my father removed the slivers of perch bones.
Eyes grew bigger to taste the mild flakes off his fingertips.
He chuckled and was amused.
I remember this.

I disrupted his rest deep in the ground.
On a rainy Welsh evening, my father
shared sea bass with me,
Salt-steamed.
Simplicity melted in our mouths.
We ate in silence.
He was proud of such a choice
over the cheery clamor of a British pub.

Aunt Bernadette's Ghosts

Lost in buried stories
on a Welsh village lane
sits a sage-green boarding home.
A near century old. Solid.
Aunt Bernadette never lived there.
She passed on her venture and legacy
to her son and he to his daughters.

Renters came.
Renters left.
Renters died in the house.
Two children's murmurs
drifted in drafts along the long corridors.
The next renters declared before leaving,
"Something strange in that house."

Aunt Bernadette buried her two children in America
before she returned to her Celtic village,
before she built the house.

The aching attic wind lingers
with no other place to carry grief.

Cousins Growing Up at the Cottage

Humble the cabin began
With a bona fide outhouse for the clan.
Some say a work in progress.
No doubt this historical place is doubly blessed.
The bungalow fills with creative quirks,
But that is how an artist's paintbrush works.
Creaky floors and screen doors,
Rooms attached like a quilt made.
Still see a breezeway and a screened patio after a few decades.
Heavy wood shutters on windows,
Sun rays enter in limbo.
The cottage is full of beds with lots of happy sleepyheads.
Sand in the sheets cause you didn't rinse your feet.
Bathroom rules were not fun.
Number one,
Nothing done.
Number two,
Flush it down.
Out in the back lay the hidden path
To the famous racetracks.
The older folks liked the smoked fish and stinky cheese
From the old country. Plug your nose, please.
The blue plastic pitcher offered lemonade.
Drink from aluminum cups or pharmaceutical glasses; it's all the same.
Whew! A glass eye cup.
Find in the cupboard the old dented measuring cup.
Lots of cooking stories for a crew
From Grandma and others in the tiny kitchen all summer through.
Crackling fires in the stove, feel the cold morning dew
With pots of percolated coffee, a brew.
Grandpa managed the potbellied wooden stove
While Grandma played troves
Of Euchre and Michigan Rummy.
Grandma's card moves were slick as honey.

Trips Around

Alpena was farther north and the big city,
With ducks in a sparkling pond; quite pretty.
Sit in the car going down the big hill,
Turn off the car while coasting to the cottage,
fun traditional thrills.
The gigantic Paul Bunyan, Babe, and Blue Ox,
Fishing in Hubbard Lake and off the docks.
Lumberjack Days in Mio.
Folks came up for the fair all the way from Ohio.
After the canoe trip on the mighty Oscoda,
We ate at Big Boys, ice cream and root beer soda.
Sturgeon Lighthouse names another venture
Harrisville State Park seemed a too-crowded adventure,
But the trip with much fan fare
Spelled visits to the bar, Slanty Shanty,
If you dared.

The Other Side

Honored Guests
Neighbors in Sauble Beach, Ontario, directly across from Harrisville,
Michigan on Lake Huron

Five generations at the Rutson Cottage cordially invite you anytime
during the summer months.

- ♣ *Barbeque chicken grilled over bed springs.*
  Don't laugh. It works.
- ♦ *A friendly, unfriendly game of croquet on*
  precarious ground.
  Unfair but everyone faces the same dilemma.
- ♥ *A sit around a campfire for s'mores stories and*
  hokey songs.
- ♠ *Learn a bizarre card game of Euchre, even by*
  Michigan standards.
  Folks around our mutual lake share history, but
  Euchre is not one.

Address
Um. You see, that's the thing. Once you arrive by boat or canoe, just ask
anyone at the Harrisville Marina or in town for the Rutson Cottage. Wear
plenty of skeeter spray and follow the horse track to the end.
Look for the first driveway on the right.

Ode to The Ojibwa Nation

A large replica of an ancient birch bark canoe hangs from the open ceiling in the humble cottage. No family memory recollects how long the canoe has been there, but somewhere in the cottage and among the wind-blown trees and clouds, the relic carves a story.

Part I

Che-Bak-Kee-Shig, (Hole-in-the-Sky),
Of strong stature, handsome.
Became Reverend John B. Silas in the White world.
Most respected in Michigan Indian affairs
More than a half a century ago.
Obtained a degree,
Worked for Bay City Municipal Light Department,
Grew into missionary work for the northeastern
Indian Methodist churches,
A proud pastor of the Mikado Indian Church.
Married an Ojibwa of much younger years,
Miss Estelle M. Squada.

Part II

Gentle ways, round face, stocky.
A visit from Mrs. Silas was as though royalty was present.
Birds chirped. Sun sparkled.
Tree roots mingled with each other.
She belonged on this land.
She was native of this land.
Admired by Grandma,
Because both felt kinship in the once
Held-fast Indian lands of Alcona County.
Admired by Grandpa,
For setting her own broken leg
In the middle of the Michigan northeastern woods.
Mrs. Silas came with bundles
Of sweetgrass baskets and other native crafts.

The three elders caught up with their news of church, family, community.
To this day, the fragrance of sweetgrass lingers
In the old cottage walls like wind beneath the wings.

Part III
Where do the three daughters, their children's children live now?
The Silases weaved memories into the fabric of the cottage family,
Five generations protected by the ancestral spirits of a First Nation.

Acknowledgements

Dr. David Hutto, *el novio*, the trusted critic
Navi, *la gata*
Johns Creek Poets
Amy Jo's Round Robin
Shiela Shinholster, book-cover design
Bobbie Christmas, editor

Navi, my writing angel, spends many hours with me at the screen.

Dearest Reader,

It means a lot to me that you read my work. I hope you found pieces that jelled with you, triggered emotions, and piqued your imagination. Or maybe you plain didn't understand the darn thing or didn't agree with the message. That is okay, too.

The essence and interpretation of each poem may change quite abruptly from one poem to another and from one day to the next. Poetry, like any artistic endeavor, is a craft and a driving force. Poetry is therapy, houses our sentiments, and quenches our imagination. I am grateful to have such a creative outlet that offers me solace, a platform when I have important things to say, a perfect reason to spend time with fellow poets and like-minded souls, or just because.

My next book endeavor is an illustrated adventure story in poetry form, which has been accepted by a publisher in Atlanta, Georgia.

Poetically Yours,

Kathy Ellis
June, 2021

Made in the USA
Columbia, SC
28 June 2021